D. LEMARESQUIER / G. PIVARD

Will you be King of England?

History through play

OREP
EDITIONS

THIS GAME BOOK OFFERS YOU THE OPPORTUNITY TO REDISCOVER HISTORY THROUGH PLAY.

IT WILL TAKE YOU BACK TO THE MIDDLE AGES, TO THE KINGDOM OF ENGLAND AND THE DUKEDOM OF NORMANDY.

WILL YOU BECOME KING OF ENGLAND?

ONLY YOU WILL KNOW AS YOU MAKE YOUR WAY THROUGH THE OBSTACLES ON EACH PAGE. AT EACH STAGE IN THE ADVENTURE, YOU WILL NEED TO MAKE THE RIGHT HISTORICAL CHOICES TO WIN « KNIGHT » POINTS. ONE OR SEVERAL OTHER GAMES WILL ALSO ENABLE YOU TO WIN « ARCHER » OR « BONUS » POINTS. THE COVER FLAP AT THE END OF THE BOOK PROVIDES A SIMPLE WAY TO COUNT YOUR POINTS AS YOU WORK YOUR WAY THROUGH THE ALBUM.

ALL OF THE SCENES AND ILLUSTRATIONS IN THIS PUBLICATION ARE FREELY INSPIRED FROM THE FAMOUS BAYEUX TAPESTRY. THIS 11TH CENTURY EMBROIDERY, UNIQUE ACROSS THE GLOBE, IS AN EXCEPTIONAL REPRESENTATION OF MEDIEVAL SOCIETY AND OF THE CONQUEST OF ENGLAND IN 1066.

Stage n°1

The adventure

Play to win 5 « knight » points

One morning in 1064, Edward the good King of England, nicknamed the Confessor, called for his advisor, Harold, to join him in the great hall of Winchester Palace where he announced, « *Noble Harold, I entrust you with a message to take to my cousin William, Duke of the Normans who lives across the sea. Tell him that, should he wish, he will become king after me; I want him to be my successor! Go now, and repeat this message to him.* »
Harold, a powerful lord, took note of his king's words.

What happened next?

A Harold left immediately without challenging the king's decision.
B He refused outright, exclaiming that no stranger would be King of England!

Answer _____

The game

Play to win 2 « archer » points

Edward has lost his hat. Help him to find it and draw it yourself.

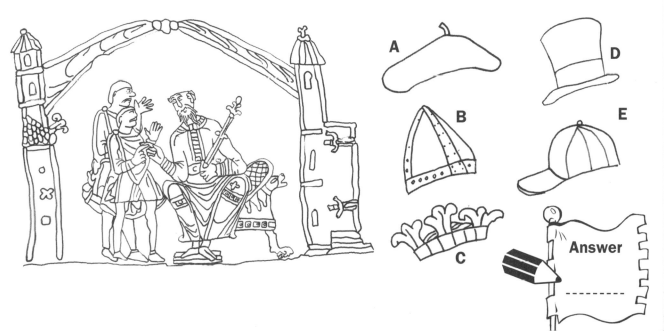

Answer _____

Stage n°2

Answers for stage n°1
The adventure: A
you win + 5 « knight » points
The game: C
you win + 2 « archer » points

 ## The adventure

Harold travelled on horseback to his land in Bosham near the coast. When he arrived, he prayed in the church, then ate in his manor house before embarking for Normandy. The English Channel crossing was trouble free until, suddenly, a terrible storm broke out.

What happened next?

**Play to win
5 « knight » points**

A Harold decided not to fight against the storm. With the strong wind in the sails, the boat drifted eastwards.

B Harold did not want to go astray from his intended route, he had to reach Normandy at all costs and deliver the message to William! The crew fought relentlessly against the fierce storm.

Answer

The game

Arrange the similar churches in pairs.
The one that's left is the genuine Bosham church.

**Play to win
3 « archer » points**

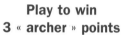

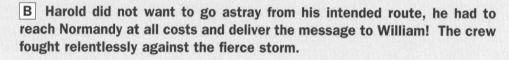

A B C D E

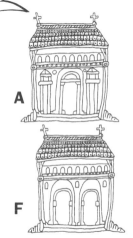 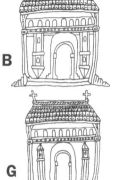 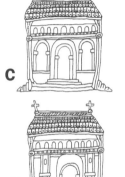  

F G H I

Answer

Bonus game

Play to win 2 « bonus » points

Draw the windy sails in the storm and the dragon head situated on the front of the ship, then colour them in.

Stage n°3

Answers for stage n°2
The adventure: A
you win + 5 « knight » points
The game: G
You win + 3 « archer » points
Bonus game: *+ 2 « bonus » points*

Early in the morning, the storm had calmed. Suddenly, a sailor, perched high up on the mast, cried out, *« Land! Land ahead! »* Indeed, a coastline was visible on the horizon. After having battled against the mighty elements all through the night, the sailors dropped anchor.

Barely had Harold set foot on the beach, when two armed men attacked him. Harold brandished his knife in self defence.

What happened next?

Play to win 5 « knight » points

A Harold was determined to fight courageously for his life. He threw himself upon his two aggressors.

B Just as Harold was preparing to resist the attack, a third man appeared on horseback and bellowed, *« I am Guy, Count of this land, surrender and you will come to no harm! »* Harold dropped his weapon.

One of these dragon heads does not have a symmetrical counterpart. Can you find it?

Play to win 3 « archer » points

Stage n°4

The adventure

In the great hall of Beaurain castle, Guy, Count of Ponthieu, said to his prisoner Harold, « *You have run aground on my shores, Englishman, and I have the right to demand a ransom in exchange for your freedom. Send one of your men to England immediately to collect money for your release!* »

What happened next?

 A Harold refused to negotiate the ransom. He believed that Guy was behaving like a pirate and an honourless man. He told him to get lost. He would wait for an opportunity to escape.

B Harold negotiated his release over several days. He lost precious time before finally meeting William and delivering Edward's message. What would his king think when he discovered the tricky situation he was in?

Play to win 3 « knight » points

Answer
‒‒‒‒‒‒‒‒

The game

Play to win 4 « archer » points

Find the deliberate mistake:
How many mistakes can you find?

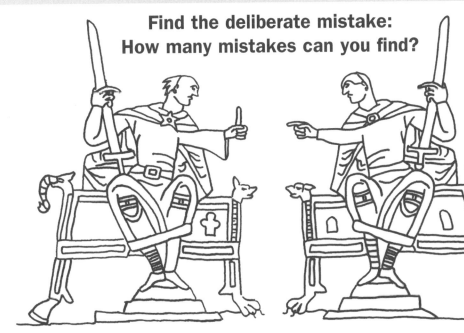

- **A** 10
- **B** 11
- **C** 12
- **D** 13

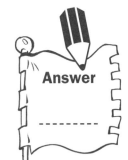
Answer
‒‒‒‒‒‒‒‒

Stage n°5

Answers for stage n°3
The adventure: B
you win + 5 « knight » points
The game: C
you win + 3 « archer » points

The adventure

A spy informed William of Harold's capture. He had him released in order to find out the reason for his visit to Normandy. To do so, he had negotiators sent to pay the ransom, then set off himself to fetch Harold and to bring him back to his castle in Rouen.

What happened next?

Play to win 5 « knight » points

A Harold was furious about the way he was treated by the Count of Ponthieu. He sought revenge. So he asked William to prepare an army to invade the Ponthieu region. Harold threatened not to deliver the message, should the Duke refuse.

B Harold could finally deliver his message to the Duke, « *Edward wishes that you succeed him to the throne of England!* ». To seal their alliance and to demonstrate his great power, William invited Harold to battle with him in Brittany.

Answer

The game

Play to win 2 « archer » points

Answer

What drawing is represented on this knight's shield?

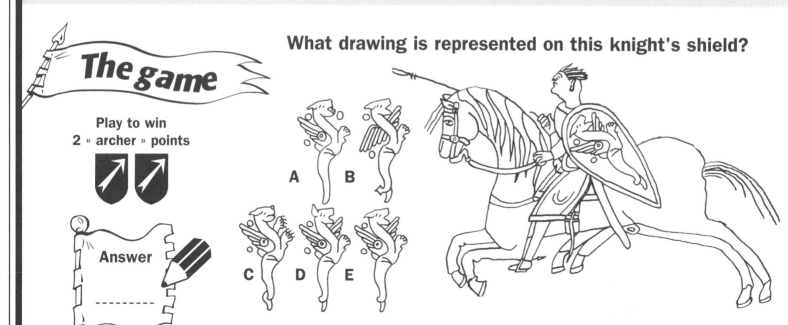

A B
C D E

Answers for stage n°4 **The adventure: B** *you win + 5 « knight » points* **The game: C** *you win + 4 « archer » points*

Bonus game

Play to win
2 « bonus » points

Draw and colour in a portrait of Harold using the model, but make your drawing symmetrical, so that he is looking towards the right.

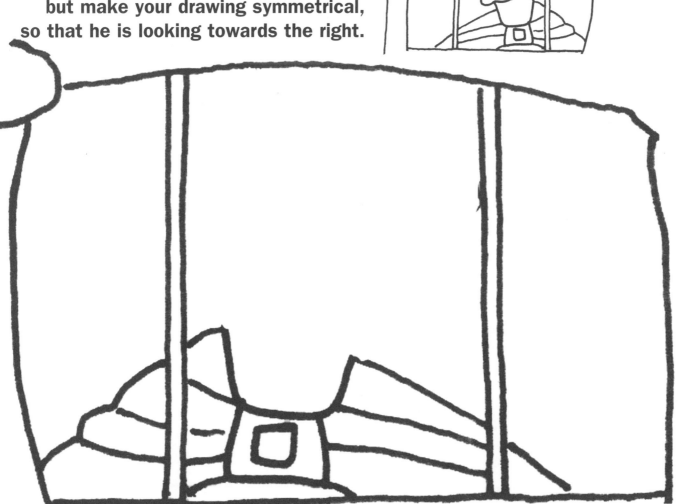

Stage n°5

Stage n°6

Answers for stage n° 5
The adventure: B
you win + 5 « knight » points
The game: E
you win + 2 « archer » points
The bonus game: *award yourself + 2 « bonus » points if you have completed your drawing*

Accompanied by Harold, Duke William led his army across the Mont-Saint-Michel bay on their way to Brittany. Close to the famous abbey, soldiers were suddenly trapped in the terrible and deadly sinking sand.

Play to win 5 « knight » points

What happened next?

A Harold noticed two men up to their waists in muddy sand. Spurred by his bravery alone, he rushed to rescue them from certain death.

B Aware of the danger, cunning Harold decided not to help the soldiers but to swerve away from the path they had taken.

Answer

One of the 4 enlargements is not part of the drawing. Can you find it?

Play to win 2 « archer » points

A    B

C    D

Answer

Bonus game

Game n° 1

Sort the horsemen into order by size, smallest first.

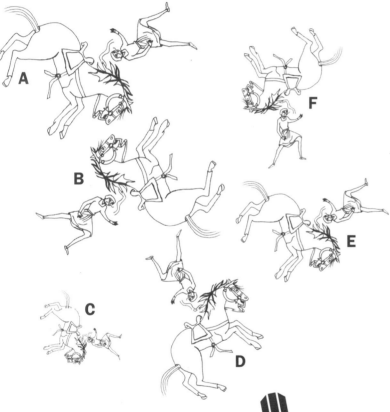

Play to win 3 « bonus » points

Answer

Game n° 2

What does this drawing represent? Find out by joining the dots.

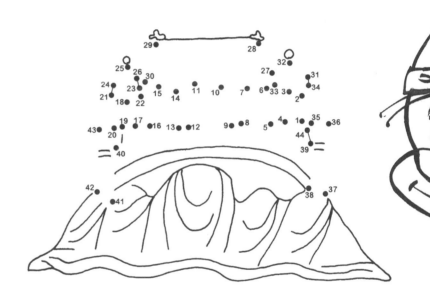

A the Chateau de Versailles
B the Mont-Saint-Michel
C Bayeux Cathedral

Play to win 1 « bonus » point

Answer

Stage n° 7

Answers for stage n° 6
The adventure: **A** you win + 5 « knight » points
The game: **D** you win + 2 « archer » points
Bonus games:
Game n° 1: **C-F-E-D-B-A** you win + 3 « bonus » points
Game n° 2: **B** you win + 1 « bonus » point

##

After having escaped the perils of the Mont-Saint-Michel bay, William's army successively attacked Dol and Rennes. And each time, Conan, the Count of Rennes, managed to escape. He sought refuge in Dinan castle which was then besieged by the Norman army. Conan was forced to hand over the town keys. The Norman expedition to Brittany had met with success!

Play to win 5 « knight » points

What happened next?

A During this campaign, Harold had proved to be very brave. He fought like a lion and, as a reward for his courage, the Duke knighted him.

B Harold did not want William to become King of England. He wanted to reign himself. So he tried to help Conan, William's enemy.

Answer

##

Find the left half to form a symmetrical Rennes mound.

Play to win 2 « archer » points

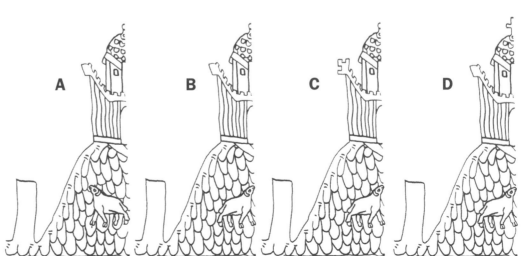

Answer

The adventure

Play to win 5 « knight » points

Harold's knighting ceremony, during which he was presented with arms, was very moving. William, Duke of Normandy, declared, « For your bravery, I give you the arms worthy of a noble and valiant knight; I declare you my brother in arms, be faithful to me and I shall help you!...»

The Norman army then travelled to Bayeux where William asked Harold to make an oath of loyalty to him.

What happened next?

A Harold swore to help William accede to the throne of England upon the death of King Edward.

B Harold thought that swearing an oath on holy relics would be like betraying God. One cannot swear loyalty to two lords at the same time. As an Englishman, Edward was the only sovereign he was prepared to acknowledge.

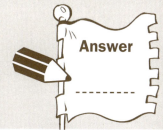

Answer

The game

Play to win 3 « archer » points

Only one of these shadows fits the castle. Draw a circle round it.

Answer

Answers for stage n° 7   **The adventure: A** *you win + 5 « knight » points*   **The game: B** *you win + 2 « archer » points*

Bonus game

Play to win 2 « bonus » points

Draw the knight using the squares to guide you.

Answers for stage n°8
The adventure: A *you win + 5 « knight » points*
The game: H *you win + 3 « archer » points*
Bonus game: If you have copied the drawing, *award yourself + 2 « bonus » points*

Stage n°9

The scene took place in Bayeux Cathedral. Harold, stood upright and swore an oath upon holy relics that were kept in the church, « I, Harold, swear my friendship to William, Duke of Normandy. Upon the death of King Edward, with the agreement of the English people I shall help him to accede to the throne and I shall be faithful to him... » Harold then returned to England to report his greatly troubled mission to his king. On the 5th of January 1066, Edward died. The English lords gathered together and decided to present Harold with the crown!

Play to win 5 « knight » points

What happened next?

A Harold was delighted to accept insisting that Edward, on his death bed, had designated him as his successor.

B Harold refused explaining that he had sworn on the holiest of Norman relics that he would let William, Duke of Normandy, become King of England. An oath made before God was not to be broken.

Answer

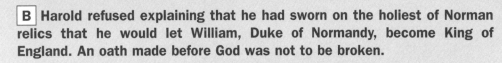

Carefully look at this scene and count the number of objects that do not belong to William the Conqueror's era.

Play to win 3 « archer » points

A	7
B	8
C	9
D	10
E	11

Answer

15

Bonus game

Play to win 3 « archer » points

Colour-maths: Do the additions
and use the answers to colour in correctly.

From 0 to 49: red　　From 60 to 69: orange　　From 80 to 89: pink
From 50 to 59: green　　From 70 to 79: black　　From 90 to 99: yellow

Stage n°10

The adventure

On the 6th of January 1066, Harold was crowned King of England in Westminster Abbey by Stigand, the Archbishop of Canterbury. The English people came in crowds to hail their new king.

Play to win 5 « knight » points

What happened next?

A A little later, a comet shot across the English skies. Could this be a foreboding? Was a catastrophe brewing?

B Later, the English saw a comet shooting through the sky. Could this be a good omen? Would Harold's reign be a happy one?

Answer _____

The game

Draw the object Harold held in his hand on the day of his coronation.

Play to win 2 « archer » points

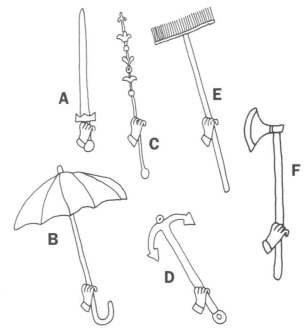

Answer _____

Stage n°11

Answers for stage n° 9
The adventure: **A** *you win + 5 « knight » points*
Le jeu : **C** *you win + 3 « archer » points*
Bonus game:
The drawing represents Harold swearing his oath
you win + 3 « bonus » points

Harold was informed of the presence of a shooting star in the English skies. Could this event herald misfortune for his kingdom? Comets are generally thought to be bad omens!... At the same time in Normandy, William, who had learned of the traitor Harold's coronation from his spies, was faced with an important decision...

Play to win 3 « knight » points

What happened next?

A William already needed many of the men from his army to control the borders of his Norman dukedom. He realised that going to England, a hostile land, to lay hands on the throne was pure madness. He would surely send his men to their death and may even lose his own territory. He gave up the idea of succeeding Edward and of becoming King of England.

B William was furious and decided to organise the greatest expedition ever seen on earth to conquer the throne he rightly believed was his. God, surely offended by Harold's perjury, could only be on the Norman side.

Answer

Help this messenger find his way to King Harold.

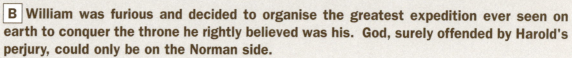

Play to win 2 « archer » points

Answer

18

Answers for stage n° 10   The adventure: **A** *you win + 5 « knight » points*   The game: **C** *you win + 2 « archer » points*

Stage n°11

Bonus game

Game n° 1

What does this drawing represent? Find out by joining the dots.

Play to win 1 « bonus » point

A	a key
B	a fish
C	a comet

Answer
_____

Game n°2   Copy this drawing using the squares to guide you.

Play to win 2 « bonus » points

19

Stage n°12

Answers for stage n° 11
The adventure: B *you win + 3 « knight » points*
The game: C *you win + 2 « archer » points*
Bonus games:
Game n° 1: C *you win + 2 « bonus » points*
Game n°2: If you have copied the drawing, *award yourself + 2 « bonus » points*

William summoned the most powerful people in his dukedom. He had a great fleet of ships built and gathered them together in the Dives estuary. Later, the fleet sailed to the Somme bay. On the evening of the 27th of September 1066, horses, weapons and food supplies were loaded on board. It was then time for the impressive army of Norman warriors and mercenaries to embark before leaving the harbour to cross the English Channel. William was on his way to conquer the throne!

What happened next?

A On the morning of the 28th of September, the Norman fleet reached the English shores. The landing of men, horses and equipment could now begin.

B In the morning, William's ship, faster than the others, arrived alone on the English shores. The duke decided to disembark immediately and to organise the landing of his army.

Play to win
5 « knight » points

Answer

Carefully look at this drawing and count the number of objects that do not belong to William the Conqueror's era.

Play to win
3 « archer » points

A	10
B	11
C	12
D	13

Answer

Bonus game

Play to win 2 « bonus » points

Turold is an enigmatic character from the Bayeux Tapestry. How many times does he appear in this drawing?

| A | 4 | B | 5 | C | 6 | D | 7 |

Answer

Stage n°12

Stage n°13

Answers for stage n° 12
The adventure: **A** *you win + 5 « knight » points*
The game: **C** *you win + 3 « archer » points*
Bonus game: **B** *you win + 2 « bonus » points*

The adventure

William's ship which was faster than the other vessels, patiently awaited the arrival of the fleet.

A massive landing was organised to frighten any English warriors who may have been in the vicinity. Norman scouts explored the surroundings and captured domestic animals to feed the hungry army. Soldiers built an entrenched camp to ensure their defence. A great feast was organised so that each and every one of them could gather strength to face the fast approaching English enemy.

Play to win 3 « knight » points

What happened next?

A William was informed of the approach of Harold's army. He realised that he was not powerful enough to invade the entire kingdom of England and that his idea to conquer this territory by force was completely mad. The men hastily rejoined their ships. They would come back later, better prepared and in greater numbers.

B Together with his brothers and his barons, William prepared a cunning battle plan making the best use of the surrounding terrain. He ordered all of his soldiers to prepare for what was sure to be a fierce battle.

Answer

The game

Count the boats.

Play to win 3 « archer » points

A	18
B	19
C	20
D	21
E	22

Answer

Bonus game

Play to win 2 « bonus » points

Colour maths : Add and colour in. What does this drawing represent?

0 to 100: yellow
101 to 200: dark green
201 to 300: light green
301 to 400: red

401 to 500: pink
501 to 600: blue
601 to 700: orange

Stage n°13

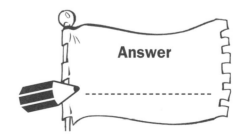

Answer

Stage n°14

Answers for stage n° 13
The adventure: **B** *you win + 3 « knight » points*
The game: **C** *you win + 3 « archer » points*
Bonus game:
The drawing represents ships being built:
you win + 2 « bonus » points

At dawn, the Normans took up position on the future battlefield, close to the town of Hastings.

What happened next?

A Hardly had the English arrived face to face with the Normans that they turned round and fled!

B The battle began; it was ferocious, and much blood was lost. Very soon, the dead bodies of warriors and their horses were strewn across the battlefield.

C William challenged Harold to a mortal duel: the winner would become the legitimate King of England!

Play to win 5 « knight » points

The game

How many crowns, soldiers, horses, shields and swords can you find?

Play to win 5 « archer » points

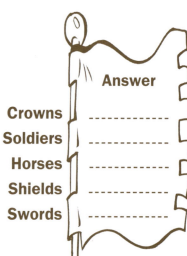

Answer
Crowns ....
Soldiers ....
Horses ....
Shields ....
Swords ....

Bonus game

Stage n°14

| Game n°1 | How many differences are there between these two horsemen? |

Play to win 3 « bonus » points

A 14
B 15
C 16

Answer

| Game n° 2 |

Take a close look at this group of horsemen.
Something's odd; can you find it? You can also colour in the drawing.

Play to win 1 « bonus » point

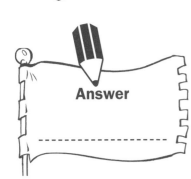

Answer

25

Stage n°15

Answers for stage n° 14
The adventure: B *you win + 5 « knight » points*
The game: Crowns: 1, Soldiers: 21, Horses: 5, Shields: 11, Swords: 10
award yourself + 1 « archer » point for each correct answer
Bonus games:
Game n° 1: A *you win + 3 « bonus » points*
Game n° 2: The horses' legs are missing *you win + 1 « bonus » point*

The Normans repeatedly attacked the English who were entrenched at the summit of Senlac Hill. Harold's men resisted and the assaulting troops came fighting back each time.

Then a terrible clamour broke out among the Norman ranks, *« William is dead!!!... »* As fast as an arrow, doubt submerged the battlefield; could Harold have defeated him?

Play to win
5 « knight » points

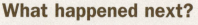

What happened next?

A William was, indeed, dead.

B The anxious Normans searched the battlefield for William's reassuring silhouette...

Answer

How many swords are there on this battlefield?

A 28
B 30
C 32
D 34

Play to win
3 « archer » points

Answer

Bonus game

Play to win 1 « bonus » point

Draw the missing sections, then colour in the drawing.

Stage n°16

Answers for stage n° 15
The adventure: **B** *you win + 5 « knight » points*
The game: **C** *you win + 3 « archer » points*
Bonus game: **If you have completed the drawing,** *award yourself + 1 « bonus » point*

William had not died. He turned towards his warriors and lifted his helmet high so that they would recognise him. The spirits of the Norman ranks were immediately raised. The duke's cavalry were boosted and, supported by the archers' arrows, they attacked the English again. The enemy defence lines were weakened. At that very moment, a group of Norman horsemen challenged Harold's personal guard: the formidable « housecarls ».

Play to win 3 « knight » points

What happened next?

A After bitter and relentless combat, most of Harold's men had fallen.

B Harold's men, fitter and familiar with the terrain, managed to fend off the Normans.

Answer

The game

One of the 5 enlargements is not part of the drawing. Can you find it?

Play to win 2 « archer » points

Answer

Bonus game

Play to win 2 « bonus » points

There are three of each of these weapons, except one. Can you find it?

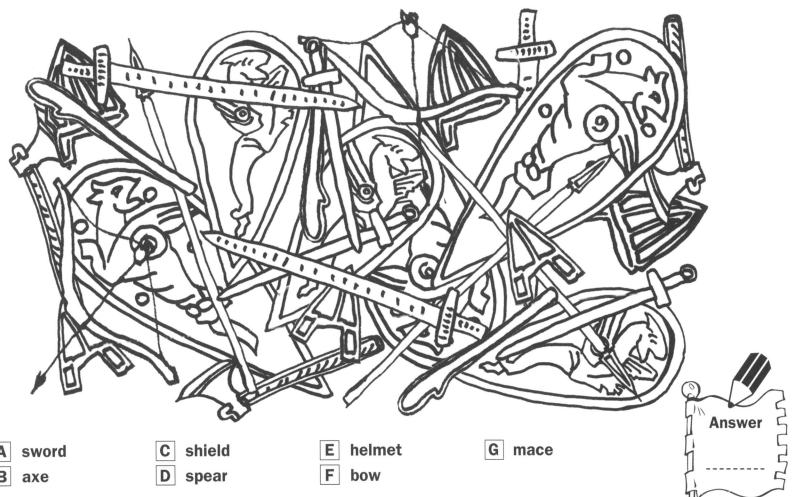

- **A** sword
- **B** axe
- **C** shield
- **D** spear
- **E** helmet
- **F** bow
- **G** mace

Answer

Stage n°16

Stage n°17

Answers for stage n° 16
The adventure: A you win + 3 « knight » points
The game: D you win + 2 « archer » points
Bonus game: F you win + 2 « bonus » points

The charging Norman horsemen drove into and knocked down Harold's guard. Suddenly, an arrow struck Harold's eye. Seriously wounded, he was in dreadful pain. At that precise moment, four Norman horsemen drew closer to kill him. Harold succumbed to their violent blows. The king is dead!...

Without their chief, the English ranks were panic-stricken. They fled the battlefield, pursued by the conqueror's cavalry. It was an absolute massacre. Robbers were already stealing arms from the many dead bodies strewn across the English countryside.

Which Norman archer is going to strike Harold's eye with an arrow?

Play to win
4 « archer » points

Answer
....

Bonus game

Play to win 3 « bonus » points

Copy a scene from the Bayeux Tapestry or create your own comic strip to complete the tapestry.

Epilogue

Answers for stage n° 17 **The game:** 5 *you win + 4 « archer » points* **Bonus game: If you have created a comic strip,** *award yourself + 3 « bonus » points*

WELL DONE, you have managed to find the real story of the conquest of England by William,
since nicknamed, the « Conqueror ».
Hence, on the 14th of October 1066, William, Duke of Normandy, defeated Harold's troops.
Two months later, on Christmas Day, William was crowned King of England in Westminster Abbey, near London.
You can see all of these historical events depicted on the famous Tapestry
in the Bayeux museum (in Calvados).

OREP
EDITIONS

15 rue de Largerie 14480 Cully
Tél. 02 31 08 31 08 - Fax. 02 31 08 31 09
E-mail: info@orep-pub.com
Web: www.orep-pub.com

In accordance with the French law n° 49-956 of the 16th of July 1949 on publications for young readers.

Graphic Design: OREP
Illustrations: Régis Hector
English translation: Heather Costil
ISBN 978-2-915762-44-0
Copyright OREP 2007
All Rights Reserved - Legal deposit: 2nd term 2007
Printed in France.